The Passover Story
A Celebration of Freedom

by **Sarah Mazor**
Illustrator **Sikandar Maganhar**

Copyright © 2018 Sarah Mazor
MazorBooks
All rights reserved.

ISBN-13:978-1986448055
ISBN-10:1986448053

Many years ago,
In the land by the Nile,
The children of Israel
Lived well for a while.

Then the Pharaoh of Egypt
Changed his ruling ways.
All the Jews became slaves,
Forced to work nights and days.

Pharaoh's patrols,
His foremen and guards,
Yelled at the slaves
And hit them quite hard,

As they hauled and they lugged
Bricks, mortar, and sand,
And built Pithom and Rameses,
Cities Pharaoh had planned.

The Jews cried and prayed,
"Please God, set us free!
Save and redeem us
From chains of slavery."

God heard their prayers,
And soon set His plan.
He got things in motion,
With Moses, the man.

"A strange choice," some said.
"Moses? That is odd.
Can the stuttering Moses,
Be the messenger of God?"

But Moses the Shepherd
Was truly born to lead.
A strong man of character,
Most people soon agreed.

Moses was a humble guy,
But fearless, bold, and smart.
A very good and kindly man,
With a warm and gentle heart.

He saw the suffering of the Jews,
The agony, and the woe.
He had to make Pharaoh see
That he must let them go.

Moses met with Pharaoh,
Without fear, he said,
"You must let my people go."
But Pharaoh shook his head.

"No, no!" he said to Moses.
"I will not let them go!
The Jewish slaves must work
So my golden treasures grow."

"You must listen," said Moses,
His message clear and strong.
"God of the Jews commands,
'Release them before long!'

And if you dare refuse,
A heavy price you'll pay.
I suggest you do as told
Or you'll regret this day."

"To me," said Pharaoh,
No one gives commands!"
And Moses, disappointed,
Left with empty hands.

But boastful Pharaoh
Was boastful no more,
Once God's ten plagues
Came straight to his door.

The Ten Plagues

The first three plagues
Were fairly severe.
There was blood, then frogs,
Then lice everywhere.

Wild beasts on the loose
Came with plague number four.
Like Lions and leopards
And foxes and boars.

Then livestock got sick
And died on the farms.
Then people got boils
On their legs and their arms.

When that didn't do it
Came plague number seven.
Huge fiery hail stones
Came down from heaven.

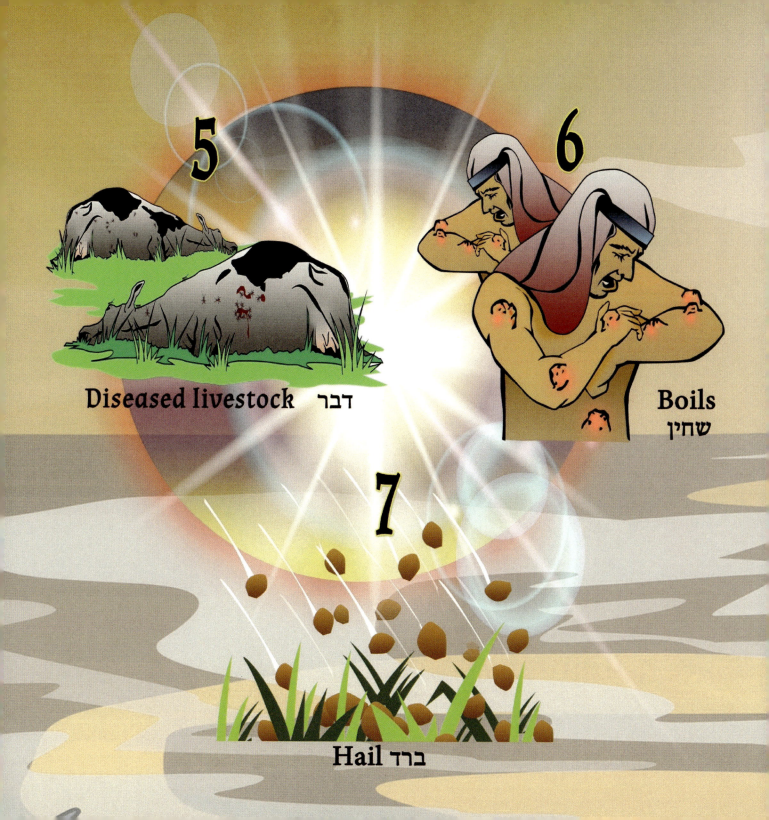

The locust, then ate
Every edible crop.
Then darkness all over
Brought all to a stop.

During each plague
Pharaoh yelled, "GO!"
But once it was over
Again he said, "NO!"

8 Locust ארבה

9 Darkness חושך

When during plague ten
The king lost his son.
And all the firstborn
Egyptians were gone.

Pharaoh cried to Moses,
"I should have listened, you know.
Take your people now!
Just take them and go!"

10

Death of First Born
מכת בכורות

Moses told his people,
"It is time to leave this place."
The tired Jewish slaves
Had a big smile on their face.

But they knew they had
Not a minute to waste.
They packed up their bags
With speed and in haste.

With no time to prepare
Delicious soft bread,
The Jews baked some matzahs,
Flat crackers, instead.

(That's why on Passover
Jews always eat,
Matzahs prepared with
Just water and wheat.)

The Israelites left quickly,
They knew that they must.
For Pharaoh was never
A man they could trust.

And a good thing they did,
For it didn't take long.
For Pharaoh to shout,
"To me they belong!"

Pharaoh sent out
A large number of groups
Of army brigades,
Commanders and troops.

But Pharaoh's great army
Could only watch the Jews flee.
As God helped His people
And split the Red Sea.

Since then, it's tradition
To celebrate each spring
The Passover Seder,
And thank the King of Kings

For the miracles performed
On land and on sea,
And for rescuing the Jews,
Once slaves, now free!

Check Out the MazorBooks Library
for more

Jewish Holidays Books for Kids

&

A Taste of Hebrew for Kids Series &
Children's Books with Good Values

www.MazorBooks.com

www.mazorbooks.wordpress.com
www.facebook.com/mazorbooks
www.twitter.com/mazorbooks

Made in the USA
Middletown, DE
03 April 2023